CHARLES KELLER

TONGUE TWISTERS

ILLUSTRATED BY RON FRITZ

Simon and Schuster Books for Young Readers
Published by Simon & Schuster Inc., New York

SIMON AND SCHUSTER BOOKS FOR YOUNG READERS

Simon & Schuster Building
Rockefeller Center
1230 Avenue of the Americas
New York, New York 10020

SIMON AND SCHUSTER BOOKS FOR YOUNG READERS
is a trademark of Simon & Schuster Inc.

Manufactured in the United States

10 9 8 7 6 5 4 3 2 1
10 9 8 7 6 5 4 3 2 1 pbk.

Library of Congress Cataloging-in-Publication Data
Keller, Charles.
Tongue twisters.
Summary: An illustrated collection of tongue twisters and other hard-to-say rhymes.
1. Tongue twisters.   [1. Tongue twisters]   I. Fritz, Ronald, ill.   II. Title.
PN6371.5.K44 1989   818'.5402 88-26448

ISBN 0-671-67123-5
ISBN 0-671-67975-9 pbk.

To Nicole and Leigh
C. K.

To my wife Martha
R. F.

Betty bought some butter, "But," she said,
"this butter's bitter, and a bit of better butter
would make a better batter." So she bought
a bit of butter better than the bitter butter,
and it made her batter better – so it was that
Betty bought a bit of better butter!

The sixth sheik's sixth sheep's sick.

Sheep shouldn't sleep in a shack.
Sheep should sleep in a shed.

Seven silly sheep slowly shuffled south.

A noise annoys an oyster, but a noisy noise annoys an oyster more.

Spiral-shelled sea snails shuffle in sea shells.

Eight apes ate eight apples.

Three tree toads tied together tried to trot to town.

Eight great gray geese grazing gaily in Greece.

A big black bug bit
a big black bear,
making the big black bear
bleed blood.

A haddock, a haddock,
a black spotted haddock.
A black spot on the
black back of
a black spotted haddock.

Peter Piper picked a peck of pickled peppers;
A peck of pickled peppers Peter Piper picked.
If Peter Piper picked a peck of pickled peppers,
Where's the peck of pickled peppers Peter Piper picked?

She sells sea shells on the seashore.
The shells she sells are sea shells, I'm sure.
And if she sells sea shells on the seashore,
Then I'm sure she sells seashore shells.

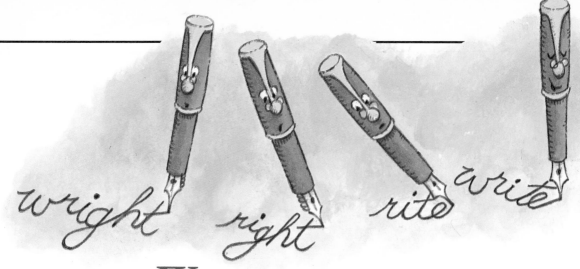

W rite, we know, if written right,
Should not be written wright or right,
Nor should it be written rite, but write,
For only then is it written right.

W hether the weather be fine,
Or whether the weather be not,
Whether the weather be cold,
Or whether the weather be hot,
We'll weather the weather,
whatever the weather,
Whether we like it or not.

Amidst the mists and coldest frosts,
With barest wrists and stoutest boasts,
He thrusts his fists against the posts
And still insists he sees the ghosts.

Lucy loosened Suzie's shoes and Suzie's shoes stayed loose while Suzie snoozed.

Isabella broke the black umbrella.

Sister Sarah shined her silver shoes for Sunday.

Sheila Shorter sought a suitor;
Sheila sought a suitor short.
Sheila's suitor's sure to suit her;
Short's the suitor Sheila sought!

Some seventy-six sad,
seasick seamen soon set sail,
seeking soothing, salty
South Sea sunshine.

Shallow ships show some signs of sinking.

Seven shy sailors salted salmon shoulder to shoulder.

Y ou've no need to light a night light
On a light night like tonight,
For a night light's light's a slight light,
And tonight's a night that's light.
When a night's light, like tonight's light,
It's really not quite right
To light night lights with their slight lights,
On a light night like tonight.

Six thick thistle sticks.

Fluffy finches flying fast.

Nimble noblemen nibbling nuts.

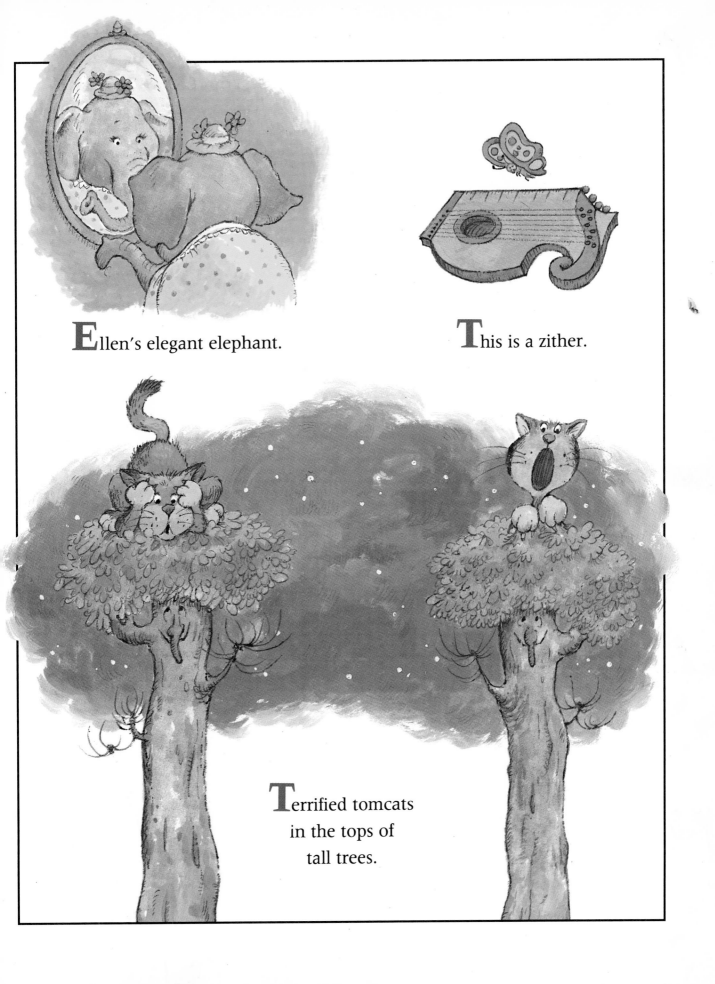

Ellen's elegant elephant.

This is a zither.

Terrified tomcats
in the tops of
tall trees.

A maid with a duster made a furious bluster
Dusting a bust in the hall.
When the bust, it was dusted,
The bust, it was busted.
The bust, it was dust —
That is all!

A tutor who tooted a flute,
Tried to teach two tooters to toot.
Said the two to the tutor,
"Is it harder to toot,
Or tutor two tooters to toot?"

Old oily Ollie oils old oily autos.

Martin met a mob of marching munching monkeys.

The bootblack brought the black book back.

Frank threw Fred three free throws.

Pop keeps a lollipop shop
and the lollipop shop keeps pop.

Sheila uttered a sharp shrill shriek and shrunk from the shriveled form that slumbered in the shadows.

Freddie's friend Eddie phoned for Freddie to fetch fruit from the farm of the famous French farmer.

Hard-hearted Harold hit Henry hard
with a hickory-handled iron hammer.
Henry howled horribly and hurriedly
hobbled home.

Round and round the rough
and ragged rock the ragged rascal ran.

How much wood could a woodchuck chuck,
If a woodchuck could chuck wood?
It would chuck as much wood as woodchuck could,
If a woodchuck could chuck wood.

A fly and a flea in a flue,
were imprisoned,
So what could they do?
Said the flea, "Let us fly."
Said the fly, "Let us flee."
So they flew through a
flaw in the flue.

"**G**o, my son, and shut the shutter."
This I heard a mother utter.
"Shutter's shut," the boy did mutter.
"I can't shut it any shutter."